Afraid? Not Me! How I Came To Love My School and the People In It

Afraid? Not Me!
How I Came to Love My School and the People In It!

by Patrice Porter and her granddaughter

© Copyright 2017 Patrice Porter All rights reserved.
No part of this book may be reproduced or transmitted in any form or by any means, including but not limited to information storage and retrieval systems, electronic, mechanical, photocopy, recording, etc. without written permission from the copyright holder. ISBN 978-1-7751178-8-9
Cover Design: Patrice Porter

Dedication

To all the Pre-K Children who have come into my classroom and also those who will be coming into my classroom.

Today is a special day!
I turn 4 years old and I can go to school.

I hugged my snuggy bunny and whispered in his ear; "Cuddles, I'm scared. I've never been to school."

"No need to be scared. I'll come with you."

"Hee Hee! I get to wear my pretty new pony dress and I've got a princess backpack for school."

Mom held one of my hands and Cuddles held the other. Off we headed to school.

Mom opened the big doors and we started down the long hallway.

Just then I heard a dog bark. I was sure he was barking at me.

"I'm not to sure about this."
Cuddles squeezed my hand and I held mom's even tighter

Mom opened a door to a room full of kids. Uhh! I see a monster under the desk and another by the cupboard. I'm sure there's monsters lurking in every corner!

Tears began to well in my eyes and were about to spill out when...

My sister Ava appeared holding two big signs.

No monstered allowed and no dogs allowed. She smiled and gave me and Cuddles a hug.

I felt better. Then our friend Terry came over with a cool magnetic chain he had been building.

He pointed to a science table which had all sorts of bright bobbles and gadgets for us to explore.

"Come on." Sis said. "I can hardly wait to show you those neat straws we can build with. Those ones I was telling you about last night."

I looked at mom and she smiled. Cuddles came with me.

I couldn't believe it. They had built a tower that was taller than me! Ava gave me a bright blue straw and showed me where to add it to the tower.

I set Cuddles down and began to build.

Mrs. P. came over to us smiling squatting beside my sister and me. "Wow! Your structure is getting really tall."

She picked up Cuddles and said he could keep watch over us safe in my backpack. She pointed to a hook on the wall beside us. It had my name on it.

"This is your hook for your jacket and backpack." said Mrs. P. "A princess! That makes this a royal pack indeed. Just perfect for your bunny."

"Everyone come to the carpet." said Mrs. P.

"Today we have someone new joining us. Her name is Patty. Let's teach her our greeting song."

♫ "Hey there neighbor,
What do you say?
Today's going to be a
wonderful day.
So clap your hands
And boogie on down.
Give a little wave
and sit right down."

"Hey there neighbor what do you say? Today's going to be a wonderful day! So clap your hands and boogie on down. Give a little wave and sit right down."

Every one had waved to me and I began to think that this was going to be a wonderful place!

Other Books by Patrice Porter

BRINGING OUT THE POTENTIAL IN CHILDREN SERIES

Volume 1 - Bringing Out the Potential In Children Writers/Authors
Bringing Out the Potential In Children Writers/Authors Workbook
Volume 2 - Bringing Out the Potential In Children Gardeners
Bringing Out the Potential In Children Gardeners Workbook
Volume 3 - Bringing Out the Potential In Children Cooks/Chefs
Bringing Out the Potential In Children Cooks/Chefs Workbook
Find them at the Full Potential Store at:
http://fullpotential.co.place
Also find this complete series along with the **Companion Workbooks** for each of the volumes on Amazon and other fine book stores.

The Coffee Break Author
Get past that barrier of having no time. Now we make time with "The Coffee Break Author" which breaks down the writing process into coffee break size sessions taking you step by step to the completion of your book.
Available at: http://bringoutthepotential.com

www.ingramcontent.com/pod-product-compliance
Lightning Source LLC
Chambersburg PA
CBHW042122040426
42450CB00002B/34